All I Need Is Jesus

Written By

Dena S. Jobes

All I Need Is Jesus

Copyright© 2019

Most scripture references (unless otherwise specified) are taken from The King James Version, The New King James Version, New International Version or The Berean Study Bible.

Editor-in-Chief: Brianna Frederick

Cover Design by: Isaiah Yarborough

Published by: Blessed Publications

All rights reserved. No portion of this book may be reproduced or transmitted in any form or by any means, including electronic, mechanical, photocopy, recording or any information storage and retrieval system without permission of author.

Table of Contents

Thank You Lord..5
Glory, Honor and Praise..................................6
According To Your Word................................8
My Painful Heart..10
Your Overwhelming Heart............................13
All I Need Is You 15
Everlasting Love..17
God's Goodness...19
Divine Deliverer...21
Divine Counselor...24
Power By His Name......................................28
His Unfailing Love...31
Daily Thankfulness..36
Abiding Savior 39
His Grace And Mercy 42

Dena S. Jobes is the Senior Pastor of Haven of Rest, Sanctuary of Praise, Inc., and the President of Haven of Rest, Fellowship of Ministries. She is also the President and Founder of One In Spirit, One In Mind Intercessory Prayer Ministry and Dena Jobes Ministries. Being mandated by God to set captives free, she loves God's people and desires for them to have a personal relationship with the Lord Jesus Christ. She strongly believes this is only obtainable through praying without ceasing. She is also a firm believer that nothing is impossible for God.

She is widely recognized as a mighty prayer warrior, anointed with the gift of intercession. Many have been set free, delivered, and healed by the power of God through the persevering, steady prayers and unwavering faith of this servant of God.

Dena S. Jobes and her husband Albert S. Jobes, walk harmoniously in all aspects of ministry and leadership. They are one in spirit and one for the Kingdom of God. They are blessed with six children and six grandchildren.

Thank You Lord

FATHER Your abundant love has ensnared me since I was conceived in my mother's womb.

YOUR love which is untainted transcends the human mind. I will never fully understand Your never ceasing love for me.

SO my heart and spirit are filled with thanksgiving. Thank You for Your unfailing love towards me.

I thank You for life, health and strength. Thank You for turning my dark places into light. Thank You for leading me into paths of righteousness for Your name's sake.

THANK You for ordering and designing my every step in You. Never cease to order my steps and I will never cease to praise You for all Your glorious acts. Amen.

Psalm 106:1 *Praise the Lord. Give thanks to the Lord, for he is good; his love endures forever.*

Glory, Honor and Praise

WONDERFUL and glorious Father I praise and honor Your great and mighty name.

YOU are the source of all my supply. Where could I live without You?

YOUR abundant love surrounds me with a never-ending desire to serve You.

OH, how I desire Your presence like a hungry man desires food.

YOUR Word have I eaten that I might live and not die.

LEAD and guide me into Your perfect will for my life, that Your glory may be revealed through my willingness to obey Your commands.

ESTABLISH my going out and coming in for Your name's sake.

I glory in Your marvelous name and praise You for your wondrous works.

THANK You Lord, thank you Lord. In Jesus' Name! Amen.

Psalm 72:19 *Praise be to his glorious name forever; may the whole earth be filled with his glory. Amen and Amen.*

Isaiah 60:1 *Arise, Shine; for thy light is come, and the glory of the LORD is risen upon thee.*

Psalm 25:5 *Lead me in thy truth, and teach me: for thou art the God of my salvation; on thee do I wait all the day.*

According To Your Word

FATHER Your loving kindness has followed me all the days of my life and my heart rejoices over it.

FATHER this is the day You have made and I will rejoice and be glad in it.

MY heart rejoices over Your power to watch over Your Word and perform it.

YOUR Word have I hid in my heart that I might not sin against thee.

ALLOW my mind to bow to Your complete Lordship as I study to show myself approved, rightly dividing the Word of Truth.

MAKE Your Word so alive in my spirit that I will always be quickened by its presence in my heart.

I praise You for Your Word being a lamp unto my feet and a light unto my path as I walk in Your will and purposes for my life.

I cannot live without You nor can I walk without Your instruction.

GUIDE me by taking my mind into deeper dimensions of Your Word that Your revelatory knowledge may become part of all my being.

I desire Your will in all that I do, so I may continually praise You through the power of Your great Word. In Jesus' name. Amen.

Psalm 119:89 *Your word, O Lord, is eternal; it stands firm in the heavens.*

Psalm 119:105 *Thy word is a lamp unto my feet, and a light unto my path.*

Isaiah 40:8 *The grass withereth, the flower fadeth: but the word of our God shall stand for ever.*

My Painful Heart

LISTEN to my complaint Father and hear the rumbling of my painful heart.

FOR the crow and buzzard have perched themselves in my presence waiting for my flesh to become a corpse.

MY heart has become enlarged in me by the pressing of my enemies to devour my soul.

THE essence of Your love has escaped their presence, leaving them bound by their own selfish desires to rob me of my joy and life.

RE-ESTABLISH Your great commandment in me to love others as You have loved me, that I might love them. MY pain I can't fully explain, but my desire for You remains the same.

HELP me to understand the great and mighty things which I knowest not that I may rest in Your desired will for my life.

BECAUSE of my desire for You, men attack me without cause. MY heart daily thirsts for Your presence to envelope me for Your glory.

I give glory and honor to Your great name Lord, for Your name is a strong tower and the righteous can run in and be safe.

MASSAGE my heart as You order my steps during this painful period of my enemies attacking me.

WHAT could have possibly been my crime to warrant my death? For only Your love has been my portion and Your character my demonstration.

ONLY You know Lord the heart of man for man's heart can be deceitfully wicked.

YOU promised that the wicked shall perish. But my desire is for Your love to cover all my sins and theirs.

I put my trust in You to deliver me from this ungodly enemy of my soul. Lord arise and allow Your love that is stronger than death to be my portion for this situation.

I love You Lord, and praise Your great name for You have and forever will do great and marvelous things for me. Praise ye the Lord. Amen.

Psalm 142:1-2 *I cry aloud to the Lord; I lift up my voice to the Lord for mercy. I pour out my complaint before him; before him I tell my trouble.*

Psalm 147:3 *He healeth the broken in heart, and bindeth up their wounds.*

Your Overwhelming Heart

WHY cry Lord when it appears no one is listening? WHY call when there is never an answer?

I cried until my eyes were dry. I called until my mouth was dry.

YET no answer was heard and no help was sent. I waited desperately for an answer and looked for help to be found.

MY agony was intense and my pain dried out my bones. Jesus help I cried, Jesus heal me I begged. I looked for Your presence and waited for Your healing touch.

BUT my cry was never heard and my call was never answered. Then I remembered that in this world there shall be many trials and tribulations.

TO reign with You I must suffer with You. To know You I must taste Your pain.

MY heart had almost fainted until I remembered Your covenant of love through Your faithful abiding Word.

YOU bid my heart when overwhelmed to be lead to the Rock which is higher than I. Thank You for being that Rock! Amen.

Psalm 34:15 *The eyes of the Lord are on the righteous and his ears are attentive to their cry.*

Psalm 34:17 *The righteous cry, and the LORD heareth, and delivereth them out of all their troubles.*

Psalm 66:17 *I cried out to him with my mouth; his praise was on my tongue.*

Psalm 46:1 *God is our protection and source of strength. He is always ready to help us in times of trouble.*

All I Need Is You

FATHER, I exalt You and I praise Your name forever and ever.

YOU are faithful to all of Your promises and loving toward all You have made.

GREAT are You Lord and mighty in power; Your understanding has no limit.

YOU delight in those who fear You, who put their hope in Your unfailing love.

FATHER You promised to give me an undivided heart and to put a new spirit within me.

FOR I desire to be corrected by You and welcome Your discipline Almighty.

I will be a blessed woman as You correct me; for You know the way that I take. I long to be taught by Your Word.

YOUR Word will not return to You void but produce a harvest of righteousness and peace in me.

BLESSED is the man You discipline, O Lord, the man You teach from the law. Teach me Lord, teach me.

FOR great is Your love toward me, and Your faithfulness endures forever. Praise the Lord! Amen.

Psalm 34:8 *Taste and see that the Lord is good; blessed is the man who takes refuge in him!*

Jeremiah 29:13 *And ye shall seek me, and find me, when ye shall search for me with all your heart.*

Everlasting Love

O LORD my heart rejoices over Your great love for me. Your love for me increases day by day and my heart is overwhelmed by it my lips repeatedly give You praise.

YOUR love towards me is patient and kind and it never keeps record of my wrongs. Thank You Jesus!

HOW could I ever live without Your love that keeps no record of my wrong, nor delights in any evil and always perseveres?

MY longing for the strength to love unconditionally is so strong I thirst for it every day. Deposit in me all I need to love as You do.

AS the sun rises and sets every new day, allow each day of my life to be filled with Your unfailing love.

YOUR love never ceases. Never allow me to cease from receiving Your untiring love nor freely giving Your love to mankind.

SURELY goodness and love will follow me all the days of my life. The earth is filled with Your love, O Lord; teach me Your decrees.

I put my hope in Your unfailing love because Your love endures forever. I praise and thank You for opening unto me the channels of Your continued love. Amen.

I John 3:1 How great is the love the Father has lavished on us, that we should be called children of God.

Proverbs 8:17 I love them that love me; and those that seek me early shall find me.

I Corinthians 8:3 But if any man love God, the same is known of him.

God's Goodness

FATHER I give You thanks with a grateful heart for Your goodness and mercy follows me all the days of my life.

YOU are forgiving and good, O Lord, abounding in love to all who call to You. I have tasted and seen that You are good Lord.

YOU are a refuge in the time of trouble. You care for those who trust in You.

FOR You, O Lord, are good, and ready to forgive my trespasses, sending them away, letting them go completely and forever. You are abundant in mercy and loving-kindness to all those who call upon You.

I will praise You, O Lord my God with all my heart and I will glorify Your name forever.

THY kingdom is an everlasting kingdom, and thy dominion endureth throughout all generations.

PRAISE ye the Lord, O give thanks unto the Lord; for he is good: for his mercy endureth forever. Amen.

Psalm 23:6 *Surely goodness and love will follow me all the days of my life, and I will dwell in the house of the Lord forever.*

Psalm 27:13 *I had fainted, unless I had believed to see the goodness of the LORD in the land of the living.*

Psalm 34:8 *O taste and see that the LORD is good: blessed is the man that trusteth in him.*

Psalm 107:21 *Oh that men would praise the LORD for his goodness, and for his wonderful works to the children of men!*

Divine Deliverer

IN You, O Lord, do I put my trust and I confidently take refuge in You. Never let me be put to shame or confusion!

DELIVER me in Your righteousness and cause me to escape the vileness of the wicked.

BOW down Your ear to me and save me from the unjust man who rejects Your Word.

BE a rock of refuge in which I can dwell and a sheltering stronghold to which I can hide from the schemes of my enemies.

RESCUE me, O Lord my God, out of the hand of the wicked and from the grasp of the jealous and ruthless man.

MY hope and my trust are complete in You as I seek Your counsel to lead me by the life and truth of Your Word.

CAST me not from Your presence as I seek to understand the ways of God. Only You know how to train my mind for the diversity of Your creation and the faithfulness of the wicked who make sport of Your great name.

O God be not far from me! O my God, make haste to help me as my heart pants day by day for Your glory to be revealed in my life.

MY heart is overwhelmed and my mind is made up to seek You that I might be found by You.

YOU said, seek ye first the kingdom of God, His righteousness and all of these things shall be added unto You.

THERE are not enough words to express my deep longing and desire to let Your holy and righteous mind dwell in me.

WHO can put into words and tell the mighty deeds of the Lord? Or who can show forth all the praise that is due Your great name?

FATHER fill me with Your presence, Your purpose and Your power, that my mind might become Your mind and my will become Your will.

TO You belong glory, honor and praise. SO I will sing praise to Your name forever and ever. Praise ye the Lord! Amen.

***II Timothy 4:18** The Lord will rescue me from every evil attack and will bring me safely to his heavenly kingdom. To him be glory forever and ever. Amen.*

***Psalm 22:11** Be not far from for trouble is near and there is none to help.*

***Psalm 71:12 (NLT)** O God don't stay away. My God please hurry to help me.*

Divine Counselor

WHAT can one say when one does not know what to say? How can one speak when the words do not come? How can one call when they have lost the will to call?

WHO can formulate words and ignite those words to be voiced, but You Lord?

I search, I seek, I cry and I call yet I seem to be dead for I cannot hear to voice my questions nor Your response to my complaints.

LORD I need thy instruction, I need thy counsel, I need thy direction and I need thy correction.

YOU possess all I need as I surrender my very being, heart, mind, soul, and spirit to Your surgical hands to purge and cleanse me from all unrighteousness.

MY extreme desire is to die in every area of my life that hinders the manifestation of Your truths by means of revelation with demonstration of Your power.

ONLY You hold the keys to unlock the barriers of my mind. Set me free from the enemies of my mind, by the power of Your Word and Your Holy Spirit.

FLUSH out all the areas of my mind that are clogged by the cares of this life and the fears of this world.

YOU and You alone Lord are the one who can deliver me from myself. Lord deliver me from every hindrance, stronghold and stumbling block in my life.

STRIP me of every thought I wrestle with every day that robs You of Your Lordship over my mind.

CREATE in me a pure heart, O God, and renew a steadfast Spirit within me. God You are my help; Lord You are the one who sustains me.

LISTEN to my prayer, O God, do not ignore my plea; hear me and answer me by the anguish of my groans.

MY thoughts trouble me and I am distraught at the voice of the enemy of my soul.

ALLOW me to crush all my enemies and overtake them; that they might be destroyed. Do not let me be put to shame, nor let my enemies triumph over me.

SHOW me Your ways, O Lord teach me, for You are God my Savior, and my hope is in You all day long. I wait in hope for You Lord; You are my helper and my shield.

IN You my heart rejoices, for I trust in Your holy name. I thank You for Your unfailing love rests upon me.

MY tongue will speak of Your righteousness and of Your praises all day long. Be glorified, honored and exalted Father God in Jesus name. Amen.

Psalm 27:7 *Hear, O Lord, when I cry with my voice: have mercy also upon me, and answer me.*

Proverbs 19:21 *Many plans are in a man's heart. But the counsel of the LORD will stand.*

Isaiah 55:8-9 *For my thoughts are not your thoughts, neither are your ways my ways, saith the LORD. For as the heavens are higher than the earth, so are my ways higher than your ways, and my thoughts than your thoughts.*

Proverbs 16:3 *Commit thy works unto the LORD, and thy thoughts shall be established.*

Proverbs 4:23 *Keep thy heart with all diligence; for out of it are the issues of life.*

Power By His Name

KING of my life, master of my soul. I glorify Your great and awesome name. At Your name every knee shall bow and every tongue confess that Jesus the Christ is Lord.

YOUR name is so great and full of such weight men tremble by Your name. Jesus Your name stands alone as the name above all names.

THERE is power in Your name, deliverance in Your name, salvation in Your name, and healing in Your name.

JESUS I worship and adore You, I honor and reverence Your name. I lift Your name up high. I decree that Your name carries the power of the heavens and the earth within it.

YOU are the King of all Kings. My heart is invigorated and exceedingly glad by the power of Your great name, the wonderful name of Jesus Christ.

JESUS I call upon thee out of the deep dimensions of my pain realizing that You have been touched by my infirmities and You are familiar with my grief.

ALL that is left for me to do with the revelations I have received about You is to praise Your matchless and powerful name Lord Jesus.

MAY my mouth, tongue and my lips never cease to render praises unto Your holy name.

YOU are the source of my supply, the provider for my every need and desire, plus the keeper of my soul so I praise Your matchless name.

GOD you be praised in the heavens and in the earth by all that You have made for the everlasting love covenant You have made unto Your people. Let all the people praise You. Amen.

Romans 1:4 and who through the Spirit of holiness was declared with power to be the Son of God by his resurrection from the dead.

Psalm 150:6 Let every thing that hath breath praise the LORD. Praise ye the LORD.

John 14:14 If ye shall ask any thing in my name, I will do it.

Romans 11:36 For of him, and through him, and to him, are all things: to whom be glory for ever. Amen.

Psalm 95:6 O Come, let us worship and bow down: let us kneel before the LORD our maker.

Philippians 4:19 But my God shall supply all your need according to his riches in glory by Christ Jesus.

His Unfailing Love

FATHER I bless and praise Your Holy name. You are so glorious and wonderful in all that You do. You are beautiful for every situation in my life.

YOUR beauty and precious love surround me with grace and mercy every day.

EACH day with You is a day filled with rich promises and rewarding pleasures.

FATHER You supply such amazing blessings that my mouth can only speak and say "I bless You Lord at all times, and Your praise shall continually be in my mouth."

MY heart is so filled with thanksgiving for Your daily loading me with rich benefits and blessings.

WHO could ever bring a charge against You except a man full of folly who never experienced Your great unlimited love?

YOUR LOVE that surpasses man's understanding is so potent that it can change evil to good, bring strength out of weakness, peace out of war, love out of hate, joy out of sadness, life out of death.

MY heart yearns for the deliverance of lost souls that are dying from the love of this world and the ignorance of Your great love for them.

IT is my prayer, in the name of Jesus, that the lost at any cost be brought out of darkness into Your marvelous light.

TRANSFORMATION mentally, emotionally, and spiritually can only happen by the power of Your unfailing love demonstrated on Calvary's cross by the shedding of Your blood.

YOU abound in love and faithfulness. No one can show love to a thousand generations but You.

IT is for all mankind to fear You Lord, to walk in all Your ways, to love You, to serve You with all their heart and soul.

BECAUSE Your love endures forever, allow Your great mercy and love to abound towards those who are struggling with the cares of this world.

O Lord, You preserve both man and beast. HOW priceless is Your unfailing LOVE! BOTH high and low among men find refuge in the shadow of Your wings.

BECAUSE Your love is better than life, pour Your powerful, transforming love upon those crying for release from the chains of darkness upon their souls. Show Your unfailing love, O Lord to them, and grant salvation.

AS Your love found me, Father let Your love find those who are lost and perplexed in their minds about You for whoever does not love does not know God, because God is love, whoever lives in love lives in God.

YOUR love is stronger than death, so allow Your banner of love to wave over the lives of the lost. Your love covers over all wrongs. Every man needs Your unfailing love.

AS I am secure in Your love, grant them the privilege to experience Your love. God You so loved the world that You gave Your only begotten Son, that whoever believes in him shall not perish but have eternal life.

YOUR steadfast love never ceases. May You direct our hearts into Your unfailing love and Christ's perseverance. It is a good thing to give thanks unto the Lord and to praise Your name, Oh, Most High!

I live that I might praise Your Holy name for ever. I praise You for Your surpassing greatness and Your free flowing love that last a lifetime. Glory and honor and praise is thine. I bless and thank You in Jesus name. Amen!

Romans 8:35-39 *Who shall separate us from the love of Christ? Shall trouble or hardship or persecution or famine or nakedness or danger or sword? As it is written: "For your sake we face death all day long; we are considered as sheep to be slaughtered. No, in all these things we are more than conquerors through him who loved us. For I am convinced that neither death nor life, neither angels nor demons, the present nor the future, nor any powers, neither height nor depth, nor anything else in all creation, will be able to separate us from the love of God that is in Christ Jesus our Lord.*

I John 4:16 *And we have known and believed the love that God hath to us. God is love; and he that dwelleth in love dwelleth in God, and God in him.*

Daily Thankfulness

FATHER I enter Your gates with thanksgiving and I enter Your courts with praise, I am thankful unto You and bless Your name.

YOUR name is a strong tower, the righteous run in and they are safe. It is a good thing to give thanks unto the Lord and to bless His Name.

I give thanks unto You Lord and call upon Your great name. I give thanks unto You and praise Your name, Oh most high.

THANK You God, for Your indescribable gift of salvation.

THANK You for Your precious gift of the Holy Ghost.

THANK You for never leaving nor forsaking me.

THANK You for being a present help in the time of trouble.

THANK You for the Word of God that is a lamp unto my feet and a light unto my path.

THANK You for mercy on whom You will have mercy.

THANK You for Your great mercy and love towards me.

THANK You for being strong and mighty, the Lord mighty in battle.

THANK You for examining my heart and my mind, for Your love is ever before me.

THANK You for being my helper; and enabling me not to be afraid of what man can do unto me.

THANK You for enabling me to rejoice in You always.

THANK You that as I take refuge in You, I am not condemned.

THANK You for being a faithful God who does no wrong and will not forsake his faithful ones.

THANK You, Lord for giving me the mind to fear You and to serve You with all my heart.

THANK You, Lord for fighting for me and giving me the mind to fight the good fight of faith.

THANK You, Lord for all You have done for me in Jesus name!

I Thessalonians 5:18 give thanks in all circumstances, for this is God's will for you in Christ Jesus.

Colossians 3:17 And whatsoever ye do in word or deed, do all in the name of the Lord Jesus giving thanks to God and the Father by him.

Abiding Savior

GLORY, honor, thanksgiving and praise I give unto You Lord Jesus.

YOUR name is greater than any name in all the world. That wonderful name of Jesus will cause every knee to bow and every tongue to confess the name of Jesus as Lord.

THERE is no one holy like You Lord. Lord You are my rock and my fortress. You are the one who searches my heart.

I am so richly blessed by the power of Your Word for Your Word is flawless and Your law is perfect.

YOU are my light and my salvation, Oh Lord and I ascribe to You glory and strength. All glory due Your holy name.

GREAT are You Lord, and most worthy of praise. I call upon thee oh Lord I call on Your great name.

YOU said, If my people, who are called by my name, will humble themselves and pray and seek my face and turn from their wicked ways, then will I hear from heaven and will forgive their sin and will heal their land.

LORD I call upon You for I desire to delight myself in You Lord and to cast all my cares on You for You are my sun and shield.

TEACH me Your way, O Lord that I embrace not the six things that You hate for Your eyes are everywhere and all of my motives are weighed by You.

LORD You are the everlasting God and my longing is to seek You while You may be found for no one shall guide me but You.

OH Lord, my strength and my fortress, You exercise kindness towards me. I desire Your Spirit Lord to rest upon me and Your glory Lord, to be revealed in my life.

LORD You are my shepherd, I shall not be in want, I will dwell in the house of the Lord forever.

FOR I have tasted and seen that You are good Lord and that You are close to the brokenhearted.

AS my everlasting Father, You are determining my steps and my help comes from You. Great are You Lord and most worthy are You of my praise. As long as I live I will praise Your name. I will forever ascribe glory, honor and praise to Your matchless and Holy name. Be forever praised and glorified master in Jesus name!

Psalm 73:28 *But as for me it is good to be near God. I have made the Sovereign Lord my refuge; I will tell of all your deeds.*

His Grace and Mercy

GREAT and mighty are you Lord. From the rising of the Sun to the going down of the same Your name is to be praised.

FROM the time of my conception in my mother's womb Your loving kindness has kept and surrounded me with Your tender mercies.

SURELY Your goodness and mercy has followed me all the days of my life. Lord, Your great mercy and love are from old.

LORD You are rich in mercy and Your mercy has made me alive in Christ even when I was dead in transgressions.

YOU will have mercy on whom you will have mercy, and you will have compassion on whom you will have compassion.

BY Your great mercy You have given me new birth into a living hope through the resurrection of Jesus Christ from the dead, and into an inheritance that can never perish, spoil or fade—kept in heaven for me.

IT is Your grace and mercy that has brought me this far. I want to thank You Lord for all You've done for me. I thank You and praise Your great and matchless name that is to be worshipped and praised forever.

AMEN.